P9-BIZ-417

Taking The History

by David Watts

For Harry & Yvette

Joy & health!

David Watts
1/NN/02
San Francisco

NIGHTSHADE PRESS

Acknowledgments: Grateful acknowledgment is given to the editors of the following magazines where these poems first appeared: *The Journal of the American Medical Association:* "Starting the IV", "MRI Scan"; *The Lancet:* "Between Illness and Recovery," "Apnea," "Elevator Talk"; *Mediphors:* "Between Hospitals"; *The Pharos:* "Diagnosis," *Slipstream:* "Cystoscopy Nurse," "Physical Exam" (republished); *The Western Journal of Medicine:* "Conscious Sedation," "Sitting in Medical Grand Rounds Thinking About My Divorce." Published under the pen name "Harvey Ellis" in *The Lancet:* "endoscopy," "toxemia of pregnancy," "restrictive," "stroke," and "taking the history".

Aired on National Public Radio's "All Things Considered" and reprinted with permission: "The Girl in the Painting by Vermeer."

The poem "MRI Scan" appeared in *Getting By: Stories of Working Lives*, Bottom Dog Press, 1996. "Starting the IV: Anesthesia" and "MRI Scan" were published in the anthology: *Uncharted Lines*, Boaz Publishing Co, 1998.

ISBN 1-879205-80-7
Editor: Carolyn Page

NIGHTSHADE PRESS
PO Box 76
Troy, Maine 04987
(207) 948-3427

First Edition

Printed in Skowhegan, Maine
by Central Maine Printing

taking the history

     we speak across language
     and still there is a story

     tell it in the gestures
     the body makes suffering

     and a pattern will emerge
     every wisdom a silhouette

     against the partition between us

For Joan

And this one for Bill
(1943—1996)

Contents:

Taking The History

Starting the IV: Anesthesia

I am good at this.
The arm bends out, the vein
lies stretched and succulent,
transparent under the sheen
of alcohol. My fingers slide
the slippery skin, tracing
engorgement.

He says he's fine
but I see the cinch
of his muscles. So I tell him
I'm the best
and he eases,
slightly.

The needle glides
under the skin, beveled tip
in its slip along the vein
where I rest it
and let him relax. It waits
like a mosquito attached
by its sucker.

I press the tip
against the bulbous channel
and the wall bends, resisting
for an instant, then,
as if capitulating, gives way
and a column of blood
enters the tubing.

I have learned not to hesitate here,
not to let fears of my own
about anesthesia, about loss
of control, get in the way.
He will want to descend
quickly, not pausing
to feel each station of detachment.
I take the control he gives me
and bring him down.

endoscopy

a little light
a little drifting music
and the body unfolds like a universe

it is asking
for this disrobing
it accepts so easily

little visions
taken like an image
half made half

rising up
from the flesh

ms

it was like his nerves
were dipped in pickling vinegar
piecemeal
starting at the periphery and spotting
in between
and it was changing
like a transforming request
a sensory overload
where some impulses make it
some don't
and that's the story
of his numbness
except that it felt like oatmeal
drying on the skin
only with oats you can see
where the damage is
they say that stress
could have started it
oh he could buy that story
and have pocket change
left over
while this moth of his nightmare
kept eating at the wool
of his nerve endings

Physical Exam

I have told her I will not
do a pelvic, so already
we are on better terms.

I have learned when best
to say this,
so as to ease her fears.

But she worries that I
will examine her breasts, perhaps
take too much pleasure
with beauty,
with softness... it's possible.

The truth is
unlike those I have loved
I do not remember the breasts
I examine. I didn't think
it would be this way,
but it is.

And I feel the opening
of possibility, it's just that
it goes unrecorded,
as if to honor
the unspoken agreement. Afterwards,

a transformation,
as if through this intimacy
we have become part
of each other,
protective of each other—Don't
misunderstand,
it's just that now
she stands close to me
and is not afraid.

stroke

lacunar and private
these are the modifiers

of the self's parameter
imagine one day forgetting

your favorite plum sauce
a little event and the circuitry

goes down freezing electrons
at the mute periphery

the center torpid
as a yogurt

little wake up calls
glowing under the fog

Coma

I awoke to a dream
and the dream was contained
and it said expanse
and institutional
walls.

No one else was sleeping
in the long Alaskan light.

The words flew over me
like snow geese.
I knew their names
only my fingers wouldn't rise
to catch them.

I could have told many things
about the underside
of language
the soft light of the body
how there are no
decisions.

With no one to hear
I thought guacamole
and raising children
and how constant the universe
is.

Between Illness and Recovery

Nothing moves but the blood
behind my ear.
Even the moment sticks

to the one before
regretting the slow pull.
It's a different kind of time

that wants to call attention
to itself. And I'm stuck here
in a room where exhaled breaths

and body sheddings wrap me
like wasp paper.
I puff oxygen

and hibernate like a hot fish
in a mud hole.
I have lived places

where time passed without restraint,
inconspicuous, uncounted,
the body lifted

in its unselfconscious dream.
But here I loll
and wait for longing

approaching like the scent of snow
on the overcoats of those who visit me,
wishing well, not wishing my place

while voices down the hall
propel the world farther away
from the place it was when I was there.

Massage

Toxic, I say
when she asks,

residue of influenza
like a fine dust

in my brain, the body
needs a washing out.

Then that fine cesura
of nothing, in which I rise

like a wing
over earth's morning,

even the letter
I'd been writing all week

for my son, diminutive—a stamp
of cornfield, patched

in the plains of Iowa.
How's the pressure?

she asks. And I imagine how
she places her body

in the arc that leans
on me, my

11

latissimus dorsi, rhomboids. . .
deep breath, she says,

paying attention to my
tension

crushed under the weight
of her will.

Sitting in Medical Grand Rounds
Thinking About My Divorce

Dr Chattergee is saying
that the heart can harm itself,
can make the wrong choices
and fail.
It has to do with receptors,
landing sites
along the wall of the cell
where hormones bring
their meticulous shapes
like messages of rescue.

But as the heart begins to fail,
he says, the receptors
deactivate—
turn their faces
to the wall. And the failing heart
fails more.

I wondered if the mind
might work that way,
choosing the wrong response,
like stepping into a mudslide,
like what happens when love fails
and we harm the ones we love.

restrictive

tricky lungs like a white rabbit
dark feathers among the face-color
a touch of shrinkage

breathing creaks like a tight box
a ship in a storm

tonight a diffuse moon

and my brother calls to tell
the news—short of breath
a poison pup
with smarts enough to worry

squeeze box with inside rot
a wheeze against the closing of the world

The Body of My Brother

First it belonged to my mother
or seemed to
stuffed into her
like a foot in a sock.
Then it took care of itself,
filling out
into home runs, high jumps.
There were times
it must have been afraid
hiding in a bunker
in South Viet Nam
having happen to it whatever it was
that makes bodies years later
jump out of bed in the middle of the night
not awake
sweating and shouting.
Last time I saw it
it was older than mine,
thinned out
by too many cigarettes
and favors given.
Now they've taken it
from the hospital bed
where it gasped out his last punch line
and put it in a box

that no one will ever see again
though we stand around it
observing gestures even death cannot remove:
head tilt, wry smile,
hands the same as my hands
crossed over his chest
as they never were in life
a few pictures and mementos
scattered around it
as if they were crumbs of a happy life.

missing Bill

your arrival was speckled with departure
the way air is folded
into stone

now the light in the room is like coffee
and the places you have left in the wall
keep changing

October will come again
and go
before your dark eyes land on me

see how the full moon startles the darkness
on the floor by my window
it will pass over us whether we see it or not

your patience is enormous and has wings
this may come as a surprise to you
but I don't think so

Circus

Word sure do get around when the circus come to town, don't it, he said, referring to the crowds of nurses and interns come to see the cowboy who wouldn't take off his boots. Only when I sleep and make love, he said, and the hospital's no place for neither.

Vernon Dalton had a heart murmur. That's fine by me, he said, five holes better than four any day—more love gets out. The problem was it gave him palpitations, extra beats, in the terms of the trade, arrhythmia. The doctors in Sonora County convinced him to come to the city to find out if it was dangerous.

In his hospital gown and boots, Vernon was hooked up to telemetry, heartbeat and misfire all sent on radio waves to the nursing station down the hall where the cardiac nurse watched for bad news.

They hooked him up to an IV and gave him Xylocaine, a drug that numbs the errant heart beat just like it does a bad tooth. Problem is, it numbs part of the brain as well—makes some people go nuts.

Vernon was lying in his bed, minding his own business (which wasn't much at the time) when one of his chest leads came unsnapped. Bells went off, lights flashed at the nursing station and Vernon looked up to see a flat line on his monitor screen.

I'm dead, he said, and closed his eyes.

And he feels himself falling backwards through space, darkness closing over him like water folding over a sinking stone. He feels something cool and attractive off to his left. He thinks he

18

hears his mother calling and he wants to go there but he's afraid he's headed to that hot place off to his right instead.

Just then the nurse walks into the room and snaps the lead back on his chest. The alarm is silenced. Heartbeats appeared on the screen. I'm alive, he said. I'm alive. . . again. I've been resurrected from the dead. I must be Jesus Christ.

Standing up in bed, boots and all, he starts reciting scripture at the top of his lungs. He points to the little old lady in the bed next to his and says, *You* are my first disciple. The nurse shuts off his Xylocaine.

It took a long time for Vernon to touch ground again. By then he had deputized 11 souls and started holding his sermon on the mount in the doctor's coffee room.

He survived it all and so did we. His heart was fine. The arrhythmia was harmless and so we sent him home. Last I heard he'd become a right Christian young man who wanted to be reunited with his mother in heaven. He got himself a night job, appearing at revivals in those big tents, the ones with the out of tune pianos and the wide-vibrato gospel choirs, telling the multitudes who came to hear, about the time he died with his boots on and came back to life.

Cystoscopy Nurse

I undress in front of you
though you have offered
a screen - Seer
Of Many Penises, I don't think
you'll remember mine.

I shed my pants like inhibitions,
stand naked, talking
as if at Pasqua's
for cappuccino, knowing
in the next moment I'll be spread
on the table.

Your sheets drape all the wrong places.
You rove the room,
pass into view between
my legs, clank
instruments in the pan,
pour water,
gather tubing, IV poles,
sponges...

My penis shrivels
like the neck of a turtle
retracting before danger.
You stretch it,
scrub it till it bobs
like the head of a scruffy kid
against his mother's washcloth.
I am sloshed and slathered.
Salined and sudsed.

It's just a job
for you, like picking parsnips
at Petrini's. You are perfect, un-
impressed as I lie here
wondering if any of the shafts you've fisted
return to you in your dreams,
risen in anger
or submission.

listening to borborigimi

a squeak under the carpet
luminal velocity

on a close curve
bulge and squish

a clothes ringer
on slow cycle

what propulsity
out of blindness

and we listen indecently
for the dark crescendo

Elevator Talk

Waiting for the elevator
I hear someone singing,
the tonality sweet
and unfamiliar. I think
of the Yangtsze River
and Three Gorges,
a house nearby, a lean-to
where Tu Fu might have stayed,
trying to get his family home.

She is leaning
against the jut of walls.
Wearing starched brown,
a plastic glove, two fingers
stuffed in a roll of toilet paper
she asks no one's permission.

The elevator comes
and together
the embarrassed and the inspired
crowd on. The interns talk
about scut work: the spinal tap,
the too-short note
in the chart,
how somebody needs to do
Mr. Gower's rectal exam.
But I am thinking about her gift,
the Chinese maid, her music.

bulemia

so sophisticated
it disappears

into its own language
just a little belch

and it's already
a physiology

masquerade
on the masquerader

even the surface doesn't know
to admit the question

MRI Scan

I arrive in a place
of strange light,
the kind
that takes away
intelligence.

I am dreamless.
I am made of the stuff
the walls are made of.

They tell me the magnet
draws particles from air
through my body,
energy that shakes the cells
and makes them cough up
their whereabouts.

I am a tube in a tube
with no exit sign,
a plastic cone
with sides that clack
and groan, my heart
shudders, my bones ache, I
could swear my skin rises
on a bed of crepitations
like tinfoil over Jiffy-Pop.

I no longer know
what is real. The whole
Van Allen Belt sucks
through my body,
flesh shimmering like atmospheres
after space wind.

And I wonder
if now the soul
should leave the body
and drift as vapor
over the ordeal of the tissues.
But then
the body would be left
alone. So I remain
and witness my dissection.

As Indians feared
the camera, knowing something
is lost there,
I wonder
if we ever are the same,
ever are,
after anything.

Between Hospitals

The rhododendrons in the patio
between hospitals
are blooming. Sheltered
from the wind
they are like you, mother,
as you lie in your bed
among the still walls
and the ministries
of doctors or students
moving to and fro like sunlight
among branches. You wait there
as your bones knit quietly
in the darkening soil of the body.

I cannot hasten
the silent matrix of cells
that gathers like estrus
before the whispering embryo,
the germinal humus
where spicules of bone
branch and grid.
You do this as you gave me birth
without any help from me.

If you were in my hospital
I would give you
my clever technologies
that chart the confident
shapes of chambers,
the generosity of oxygen
in the tissues, the passionate flow
of fluids.
I would give you my art

and this patio, elevated
like the Langtang Valley
in the Himalayas,
where rhododendrons search
the tall pines for the light
that drifts below them.
  I watch the blossoms,
they are like tissue, lacy,
durable. The leaves spread.
Even in shelter they quiver.

We are growing older.

diagnosis

he lay like porcelain
in his bed
the room heavy

with light
and the rasp
of breathing

only the surface
 rippled
as I entered

my hands
holding unwanted telegrams
choosing what to deliver

Conscious Sedation

She says
she doesn't want
to remember
anything.
But she is young,
anxious—
she will be hard
to sedate.
She will not trust me
enough.
She will rise up
against
the cloak of numbness.

I joke
about the "Joy Juice"
I will push
through her vein—and do it
not slow, but
twice as fast.
She says the room
just moved down
and I say
"It's the medicine."
A smile that fades
and she falls not to rest
but beyond,
to the place where
anxiety is,
then bubbles

back, "My feet
are hazy."
"It's the medicine,"
I say—a
smile, a fade
and a bouncing back: "I don't want
to be here when I'm here...

if you know what I mean."

More valium,
more demerol.
She doesn't speak
now

but her heart quickens
against the fog
and I know
when I touch her
she will rise up. . .

so I wait

until the mantle is heavy,
until it smothers even
the quick breath of fear

and I can begin.

July 16th

Hot. But the air
is still clean.
Out my window
Golden Gate Park
looks like paste-ups
on plexi-glass.
Mario is laughing
the kind of laughter he gets
from release, asking questions
he's stored on a little
white crumple, not needing
answers, the paper
disgorging itself
for its own pleasure.
His joy
simply to resolve these accumulations,
5 minutes and he'll be gone,
anxiety gone,
though his lung cancer surgery
races in
next week. Postponed,
he says, my fault, son wanted
to be there.
        Outside,
heat rises. Old people
are breathing hard.
The globe warms
beyond worrisome and I practice
medicine as I always have,
assuming we

will go on.
I am thinking redwoods,
new plantings, a glass
of chardonnay,
recovery for the scars we make
cutting our way.
Tomorrow
I will cringe a little
at the news,
do a few endoscopies,
remember Mario's tumor,
chirping
in the tree of his lungs,
its foothold
on the edge of his breath.

leukemia

there was a sound
like vertical ripping
then sparks of tissue
in a cleft of air

I had not expected
this news he said
lymphocytes failing
under the surface
of surfaces   wine sap

draining
crankcase out of oil
and millions and swarms
of pocking dust
like virus

Late February

This morning winter clear.
Plum blossoms on the ground
like frost flakes. And my friend lies still

in the ICU,
where his doctors work him
like a puzzle. Snowmelt.

Buttercurd sky. They say
don't drive and write poetry
at the same time--my mortality

the same as his mortality,
car crash—driver impaled
on a steel metaphor. Even so,

I turn to check the woman jogger
for signs of beauty.
Just a hint of spring in this cold air.

Two Edges

Haze of thinned-out paint
and behind it a city. Jut and chink,
pushing against the canvas back.

When traffic stops
you can feel the bridge move, waves
in the span. Earthquake. Like that.

They say the golf course was a pond
of soil and green. Tsunami
jamming across, shaking out

a carpet. Imagine, teeing off
in a Fun House, building as we do
on the push of earth. The jumper,

mid-span, shrieking "The city so close
it wants me. . ." less lonely
than oceanside. Solitude that steep.

She's said it so often
the weight of meaning lifts off
the words: "I don't want

to live anymore. . ." Scribble
in the chart. The phone call
to a responsible adult and

the wormhole in her atmosphere
still sucks. Crab shell. Cicada.
Crust following departure.

The edge we choose and the one
that chooses us. Particles of haze
in the rising sun.

Chronic Pain Syndrome

There was heat in the wound,
rising from the cold place
where the surgeon separated the body
for its grateful assault—
the arteries choked
with lust and butter fat,
the myofibrils hungry
in the dark chambers of the heart's
quick engine.

Aqueducts of mercy the surgeon
brought, pipes of blood
and a brand new scar
with an attitude. Wuss,
we said, but a breathless pain
suckled the breast
that had no milk, pouty now
with discontent.

              No X-ray
saw this complaint, saw
what got him Prozak
and trips to the city
with no salve but the medicinal act
of travel. But then,
a specter rose, unshielding,
spurning the cloak
of its own beginnings
like a bloody amaryllis rising
from his chest,

errant embryo unjettisoned
now self-making, in
the body, as the body's worst child.

                              Our belief
in disbelief now shaken,
we scurry to needle
and register, to pronounce
and gather what oxygen will come
late to his request,
late to his pain the prophet
of the coming of the flesh, relieved
that it's finally over,
afraid that it's finally over.

Antonio

He hisses through
his tracheostomy
as his daughter does
the talking.
She tells me
about his smoking,
his emphysema, the
operation that took away
his speech.

His fingertip
covers the red ring
at his neck
as he heaves
a few words:
"I want you
to be my
doctor
I want you

to treat me
as a friend. . ."

He is family now
and I see it will not
be easy.

I examine him.
I study him.
I learn his future.

His daughter tells me
not to say
what will come.

Now he sits
and smiles
and thanks me
as I do not tell him
everything I know.

But I am troubled.

He wears a small
Italian hat. He
is proud of
his family.
He says, "I

am so glad to
be here with you."
He says to me, "Doctor,
you have too much

to think about
to worry so hard
for me."

When Edith Got Her Cancer

She was aware that we were aware
of her, drifting
among her recovering patients
like a saint.

At her good-bye party
we watched the movie of her death
in our heads,
mad to be helpless. She

was serving cake,
tending our wounds.

nodule

pop up
unexpected kernel

undulating in a fleshy universe
like a quasar

I feel it glow
          in the unholy light
          along the undeclared path
smaller bigger   looming

tiny as a pea under a mattress

going with

I don't feel like rising to the pain
where it hovers above the bed

let it be there

among the molecules and currents
that fly from passing bodies

I will sink

into the bed sheets with their
laundry aromas

they alone comfort me

as desire drops through me
like a sinker

The Girl in the Painting by Vermeer

Ten o'clock Monday morning and she's waiting for me, my new patient, a woman who looks younger than her age of 35. She almost curtsies as she shakes my hand. She wears a light tweed suit that reminds me of Easter Sunday in Central Texas.

She has a quick laugh that juts into conversation with surprising speed and at unexpected places, as if she's embarrassed to be speaking out loud. She's a violinist, teaches a large clutch of students and is frequently tired but blames it on her heavy concert schedule. She's lost weight. No other symptoms. Oh yes, night sweats, drenching. Another doctor found something in her liver and she wants to know what I think.

In the exam room she reaches down and pats her belly. Do you see it? Do you see my hemablob? Your what? My hemablob. That's the name I gave it. She laughs. And there, out her side, a large bump protrudes, lifting the skin over it like a mound of soil over something buried. Holy cow, I think to myself. That thing's huge. She's looking up at me. Hemablob, I say. It's a great name.

We run a few tests. She's giving a lesson when I call with an update and a plan. She doesn't ask questions, just says, It's a mind boggle.

I schedule a colonoscopy. Two seconds in and I find it. The nurse groans as the lens picks up the unmistakable fleshy, crumbling mass, plastered to the side of the rectum like a fungus gone mad. The room grows quiet, as if we were standing around the embers of a house burned down, kicking the cinders aimlessly.

45

I look down at her lying on the table. She looks young and perfect, relaxed in a posture of grace like a girl in a painting by Vermeer. But I know her body's ruined, rotting from the inside out.

In recovery I tell her I found it. She says it makes sense. She's been thinking there might have been a little pain, a little bleeding. I'm sorry for the trouble I caused you, she says.

She decides to move back to New Haven to be close to her friends. I call her at home the next day. Her voice still has that light lift I heard the first time we met. I say I wish I could have found something nicer. She laughs and thanks me for picking up on her crazy way of communicating. I do violin all day, she says. I'm not very good with words.

There came a little silence in which I could not say good luck, because I knew she wasn't going to have any. We stayed on the line a while, holding on to our silence, letting it run a few saturated seconds. . . then broke the connection as we knew we must.

toxemia of pregnancy

how to score this hour
how to crawl behind the glass
        of the washing machine
and be with the motion of the clothes

that flowering pigeon
belief knuckle
the movement unseen behind a curtain

whispering show show
        show me the key to the chamber

the egg shell has a fever
a complaint at the tight junction

and I watch you swell like a yeast bread
counting the seconds baking

sleeping with toxemia

I don't think she'll wake
me slipping into bed
the weight of her breath
too heavy

she carries a muffin
yeast and honey
that leaks sweet sap in her body
and sleep will not do
to fix it   sleep

oozes   hands
 stop
and start their restless search even I
cannot rest

in the amber glow of worry

Apnea

They said it was normal
for premature infants to stop breathing
sometimes.
And though I'm sure they meant to reassure
it didn't feel like comfort, exactly.
If I thought about it from a place
outside the moment
I might believe
he would be all right.
But to see this small baby
not breathing...

I said I was afraid
we hadn't done enough
to make him want
to live
in this place of raw light,
plastic isolettes,
oxygen streaming
through the silicon tubing.

So I sit beside him
and make small human noises
against the whir and whine
of intensive care:

I clear my throat,
clack my tongue,
I make those "Oh my soul" sounds
you understand in conversation
without making out the words.
I wrap my palm
around his rump
so he can feel
the warmth of my hand
claiming him,
rocking him slowly
into the family.

Photo By: Joan Baranow

David Watts lives in Mill Valley, California, with his wife, Joan Baranow, also a poet, and their excellent son, Duston. Dr. Watts teaches at the University of California San Francisco medical school and at the Fromm Institute of USF. His previous books include *Spring's Boy* and *Slow Walking at Jenner-by-the-Sea*. He is a musician and media host, and an occasional commentator on National Public Radio's "All Things Considered."